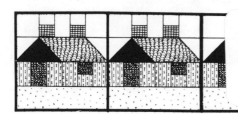

Little Patchwork Things

Nancy Donahue

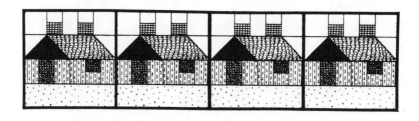

I wish to dedicate this book to all quilters who are looking for new horizons; to Joyce Kelly, Mary Hoge, Cheri Bradley and Jackie Slopko for encouragement, assistance and generous sharing of talents in the preparation of this book; to my students who modeled the clothing so beautifully.

Published by The Dicmar Publishing Company
P.O. Box 3533, Washington, DC 20007
(202) 338-2049

ISBN 0-933165-00-5

Other Dicmar Publications: The Whole Quilt Shop Directory, Butterflies, Shadow Trapunto, The Quilt-As-You-Go Guide, Kentucky Quilts 1800-1900.

Preface

The wonderful world of miniature patchwork beckons to you in the form of new and exciting challenges. It challenges you to sew tiny patches with confidence perhaps for the first time, to use all of those little scraps you've been saving for so long, to embark upon a wide variety of intriguing patchwork projects and to delight in the feeling of success over the mastery of making Little Patchwork Things.

The dainty size of the three inch quilt blocks ideally suits them for elegant clothing trims, quilt borders and the many patterns and ideas included in these pages. And, last but not least, you will enjoy the fascinating challenge of designing and making your own Little Patchwork Things.

Nancy Donahue
Hacienda Heights, California

Contents

PATTERN PREPARATION

Most of the pattern pieces you will be using for making the three inch quilt blocks are very small. The patterns should be made from a sturdy material to insure accuracy and ease of tracing and handling. I use acetate for constructing all of my patterns. Acetate never wears out and it provides a sharp edge for the pencil during tracing. It is sold at stationery and hobby stores in clear or opaque sheets.

To make a pattern, begin with a paper pattern which you have either drawn, traced or photo copied. When you use a photo copier be sure to recheck the size of the pattern afterward as some copiers will distort the original size. Cut out the paper pattern leaving approximately ¼ inch of paper extending beyond the pattern line.

Opaque Acetate Pattern. One side of the opaque acetate has a rough surface. You will be able to trace the pattern directly onto this rough side. With scissors, cut out the pattern on the lines. Cut slowly and carefully as it is not advisable to make adjustments on an acetate pattern after cutting. The cutting instructions may be written directly onto the acetate pattern.

Clear Acetate Pattern. Use rubber cement to glue the paper pattern onto the acetate. I prefer rubber cement for patternmaking because it does not wrinkle or bubble the paper. Any alteration of this kind will change the original size of the pattern. Cut out the pattern with scissors. Leave the paper pattern on the acetate for writing the cutting instructions and easier visibility.

FABRIC SELECTION

All of the fabric used in three inch quilt blocks will be cut into fairly small pieces. The prints you choose are an important factor in the appearance of the blocks.

Tiny and medium overall prints and tiny prints with a lot of solid background are the most suitable for miniature patchwork because they match the scale of the pattern pieces.

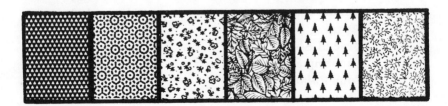

A good balance of lights and darks and small and medium prints will help to set off individual pieces within the block. A medium sized flower or design centered on the quilt pattern will create an interesting focal point.

Polka dots come in handy when you need a pattern to go between a print and a solid. They are particularly useful in blocks which call for three or more fabrics. Use only the smallest polka dots available as larger dots will appear too intense.

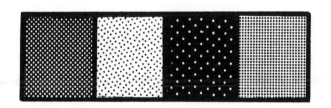

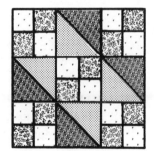

Road to California

Narrow print stripes and plain stripes may be used nicely in three inch blocks. Placed as a divider between prints, stripes make an interesting accent.

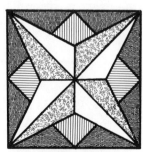

Little Star

It is not advisable to use large prints for miniature patchwork. They tend to appear chopped up when they are cut into small pieces and will detract from the design continuity of the other fabrics used in the block.

TRACING THE PATTERNS

Place a 9 x 11 inch piece of #120 sandpaper under the fabric when you begin to trace the patterns. The sandpaper keeps the fabric from sliding around on the table and aides in tracing darker and more distinct seamlines and corners.

With a sharp #2 pencil, trace around the pattern on the wrong side of the fabric. Trace the corners carefully as they will need to be well defined. Allow approximately ¼ inch seam allowance around each piece as you trace it. On dark fabrics, when you cannot see your lead pencil line clearly, use a yellow Prismacolor art pencil. Be sure to keep the art pencil sharp at all times in order to maintain a distinct and narrow seamline. Art supply and some stationery stores carry art pencils. Cut out each piece adding ¼ inch seam allowance or more. The ¼ inch seam allowance does not need to be measured.

When the letter "R" is used on a pattern, it means to "reverse" the pattern. First, transfer the grainline to the back of the pattern placing it in the exact position used on the pattern front. To trace the reverse pieces, turn the pattern over on the back.

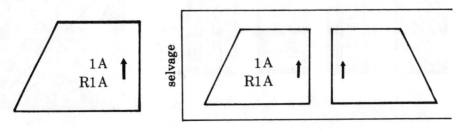

LAYOUT

Cut a 7 x 7 inch square of scrap fabric. When you have finished cutting out the quilt block, lay out each piece on the square of fabric in its proper position allowing for seams. Next, pin each piece onto the square. This is an excellent way to keep all of the little pieces in tow and it is also a great timesaver. Your patchwork will be ready for you to unpin from the square and sew at any time and it will be conveniently organized to carry in your bag wherever you go.

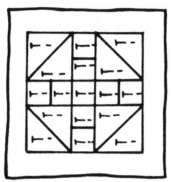

PATTERN STORAGE

Plastic seal top bags, 7 x 8 inches, are ideal for storing miniature patterns. The clear plastic aides in locating tiny patterns quickly and easily and the seal top keeps them from falling out and getting lost. You will find seal top bags at markets in the lunch bag section.

PIECING THE BLOCKS.

I prefer to piece the miniatures by hand. The short seams require only a few stitches from one end to the other which lends well to hand piecing (see page 12). If you wish to do machine piecing, choose patterns which have the most long, straight seams (see page 14).

To determine the order of piecing a block, look at a picture of the block or the laid out pieces. Most quilt blocks are either pieced in rows or units.

To make row blocks, the individual rows are pieced first then joined together.

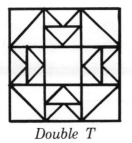

Double T

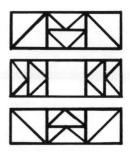

For unit blocks, piece each unit and join them to the other complete units.

Queen Charlotte's
Crown

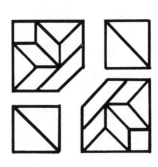

Some blocks are pieced first and then appliqued to a backing using the blindstitch (see page 14).

Grandmother's Flower
Garden

PRESSING

Press the block when it is finished. On the wrong side, press all of the seams to one side. On the right side, press until the fabric no longer rolls back over the seams. I like to use a folded bath towel on the ironing board for pressing three inch quilt blocks.

MEASURING

Measure all of your finished blocks before proceeding with your project. They should all be the same finished size to insure straight rows. Forcing blocks of varying sizes to fit together is like forcing the wrong pieces of a puzzle into position.

After pressing the block, measure it. Make a 3 x 3 inch acetate measuring template (see page 104). To make the acetate measuring template, remove the paper immediately after cutting out the acetate square. It is easier to measure when you can see through the acetate.

On the wrong side of the block, match the template to the pencil seamlines as closely as possible. If your seamlines are slightly inaccurate, center the template over them and trace new lines. Make a pencil slash line on the old seamlines to avoid confusing them later when you are sewing the blocks together.

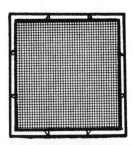 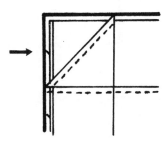

Stitches

HAND PIECING

With right sides together, put point of pin through corner seamline of both pieces. Repeat for opposite corner. Place more pins ½ inch apart from the center out matching seamlines of both pieces.

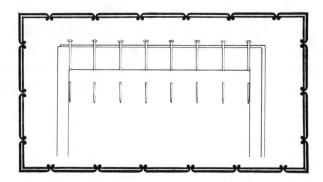

Take tiny running stitches between the first and last pins. Backstitch every six or eight stitches.

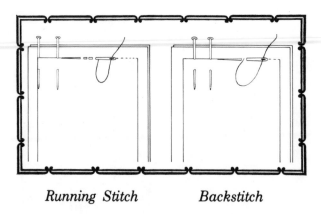

Running Stitch   *Backstitch*

To sew one row to another, pin corners first. Next, match seams by pinning on pencil seamline next to seam on both pieces. Pin rest of row ½ inch apart matching seamlines.

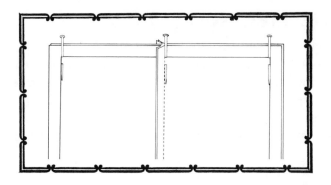

Approaching the seam, hold seam allowances of both pieces to left. At seam, make a knot but do not cut thread. Put needle through seam allowance of top piece close to knot and draw through to other side.

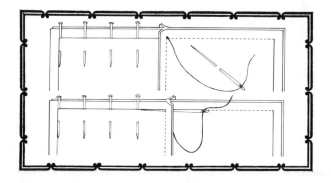

Fold both seam allowances to right side and make another knot next to seam then continue stitching. Trim seam to ⅛ inch for quilting. Press seams to one side when quilt block is finished.

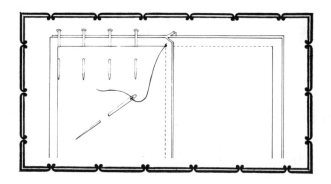

MACHINE PIECING

Matching seamlines, pin corners and pin every inch across seamline. Set stitch length at 10 to 12 stitches per inch. Begin and end stitching at raw edge and remove pins just before you come to them. Trim seam to ⅛ inch for quilting. Press seam to one side after stitching each piece.

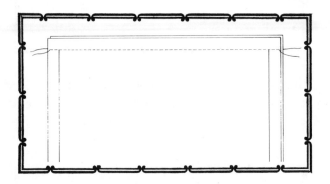

To machine piece diamonds, rhomboids, hexagons and inside corners of triangles and squares, stitch from one corner penciled seamline to the other starting and ending with backstitch. Trim seams to ⅛ inch for quilting.

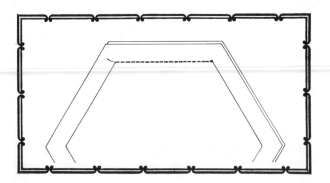

BLINDSTITCH

To blindstitch for appliqueing onto a backing, thread baste first. For hemming, basting is not required.

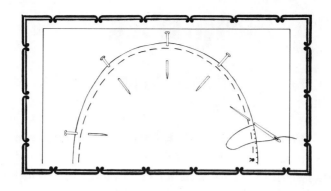

OUTLINE STITCH

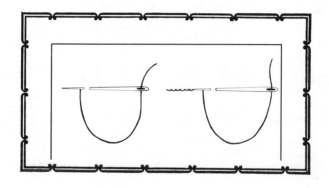

SATIN STITCH

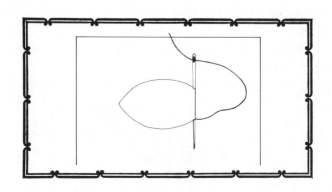

Ruffles

MATERIAL FOR GATHERED EYELET RUFFLE. Measure perimeter of pillow plus five inches.

MATERIAL FOR ONE RUFFLE. Measure perimeter of pillow and double it for length of ruffle. (Ruffle will be cut across width of fabric.) Divide ruffle length by 44 for number of rows needed. Width of rows will be the cutting width shown on pattern cutting directions or double the finished width of desired ruffle plus ½ inch.

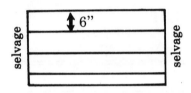

GATHERED EYELET RUFFLE

Beginning in center of one side of pillow top, with right sides together baste eyelet to pillow top leaving 1½ inches of eyelet extending beyond basting at start and end. Allow a little extra fullness in corners and round corners slightly.

With right sides together, sew ends together at point where they meet. Trim one seam allowance to ½ inch and the other to ⅛ inch. Fold under ¼ inch on widest seam allowance and place over ⅛ inch seam allowance. Stitch close to folded edge. Sew ruffle to pillow top just below eyelet binding. To keep lower edge of ruffle and gathers in place while sewing the back, thread baste around inside edge of ruffle.

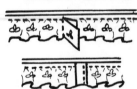

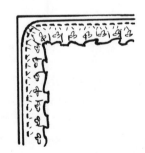

Assembly. With right sides together, sew back to pillow top just below previous stitching. Sew on three sides and 1½ inches in from each corner on fourth side to leave an opening for turning. Turn to right side and check to see that ruffle has not been caught in stitching. Turn back to wrong side, trim seams and corners. Turn to right side again.

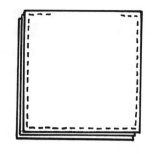

ONE RUFFLE

With right sides together, sew ruffle strips together with ¼ inch seam. Sew ends together to form a circle. Press seams open.

Fold fabric in half lengthwise and press. Divide ruffle into four equal parts and mark each section with a pin.

Between one section of pin markers, make a double row of machine gathering stitches ¼ inch and ⅜ inch from raw edge. Stop each row of stitching at end pin marker, remove fabric from machine and cut thread. Repeat for other sections. Knot all threads on left end of each section.

With a pin, mark center of each side of pillow top.

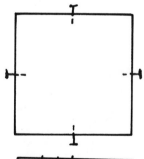

Gather one section of ruffle to the approximate size of one section of pillow top. Matching markers, pin ruffle to one section. Adjust gathers to fit between markers. Allow a little extra fullness in corner and round corner slightly. Tie off gathering thread when ruffle section is pinned in place. Repeat for other sections. Sew ruffle just

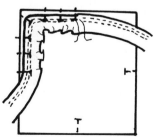

inside ¼ inch row of gathering stitches. To keep
lower edge of ruffle and gathers in place while
sewing the back, thread baste around inside edge
of ruffle. Assembly. (See Gathered Eyelet Ruffle.)

TWO RUFFLES

The outer ruffle should be 1 to 1½ inches wider
than the inner ruffle. Sew eyelet ruffle to pillow
top (see Gathered Eyelet Ruffle). Baste around
lower edge of ruffle. Sew outer ruffle over eyelet
(see One Ruffle). Baste around lower edge of
ruffle. Assembly. (See Gathered Eyelet Ruffle.)

Stuffing Pillows

MATERIAL.

Pillow Size	5 or 6 oz. bonded polyester batting, 48 inches wide
12 inch	1 yd.
15 inch	1½ yds.
18 inch	2 yds.
21 inch	2½ yds.

CUTTING. 5 batting ½ inch smaller than your finished pillow

3 batting four inches smaller than the five pieces

3 batting three inches smaller than the last three pieces

4 batting 6 x 8 inches

STUFFING. Fold the largest pieces of batting in half all together. Insert batting into pillow as far as possible. Unfold and smooth out.

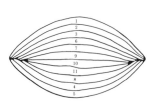

Fold the next largest pieces of batting in half all together. Split previous batting three layers on top, two layers on bottom. Insert smaller batting between the first. Unfold and smooth out. Repeat for next size batting inserting it between last group and smoothing out.

Roll up one 6 x 8 inch batting across the width. Insert through the middle layers of batting placing roll diagonally into corner. Repeat for rest of corners.

CLOSING. Turn under seam allowance on opening and pin baste starting in the middle. Center pins to right and left of middle ending with pins every ½ inch. Close opening with blindstitch (see page 14).

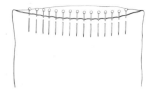

Vest Trims

TWELVE MISSOURI DAISY BLOCKS

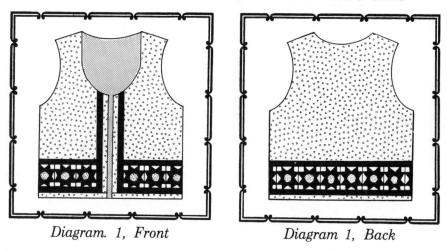

Diagram. 1, Front   *Diagram 1, Back*

Color Plate Page 55

TWELVE ASSORTED BLOCKS

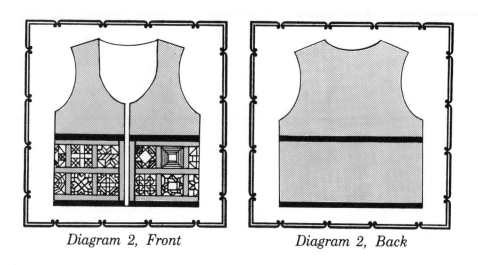

Diagram 2, Front   *Diagram 2, Back*

Color Plate Page 59

TWELVE ASSORTED BLOCKS

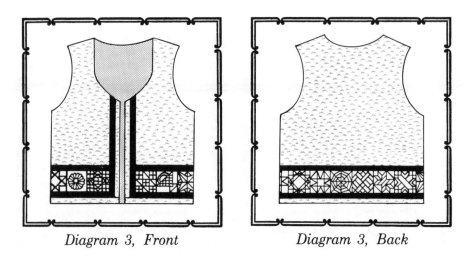

Diagram 3, Front

Diagram 3, Back

Color Plate Page 62

SIX ASSORTED BLOCKS

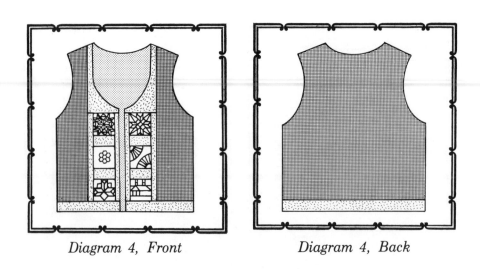

Diagram 4, Front

Diagram 4, Back

Color Plate Page 61

SIX QUEEN CHARLOTTE'S CROWN BLOCKS

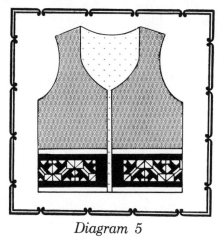

Diagram 5

Color Plate Page 58

Vest Trims

SIZE. Small.

PATTERN. Enlarge*Patches of Joy Laurie Vest front and back pattern A; innerfacing pattern B; for vest diagram 4 only, pattern C – ½ inch seam allowance included except where otherwise indicated.

1 sq. = 2 in.

½ in. seam allowance included except where otherwise indicated

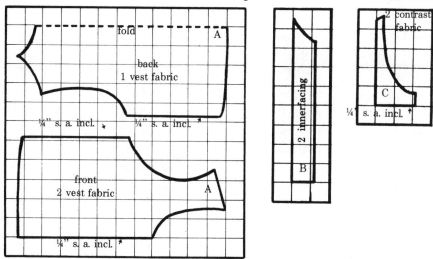

*Patches of Joy, 8050 SW Wareham Cir., Portland, OR 97223
  Side seams straightened to eliminate taper, front and side seams reduced to ¼ inch.

MATERIAL FOR ALL VESTS. ¾ yd. each lining and vest; ¼ yd. heavyweight or mediumweight innerfacing; ⅛ yd. for each color border; ⅛ yd. each fabric needed for blocks according to trim you are making (vest and lining fabric may also be repeated in the blocks).

CUTTING. Add ¼ inch seam allowance on all blocks and borders. Diagrams 1 through 5 vest and lining pattern A–½ inch seam allowance included except where otherwise indicated; pattern B innerfacing–½ inch seam allowance included; pattern C contrast fabric for vest diagram 4 only–½ inch seam allowance included except where otherwise indicated.

Diagram 1. Cut twelve Missouri Daisy blocks (see page 95); two each ⅜ x 13½ inch vest front borders and front contrasting borders; two ⅜ x 9¾ inch front vest borders; four ⅜ x 9 inch front contrast borders; one ⅜ x 18 inch back vest border; two ⅜ x 18 inch back contrast borders.

Diagram 2. Cut blocks, one each: Double T (see page 91); Bachelor's Puzzle (see page 88); Queen Charlotte's Crown (see page 97); Night and Noon (see page 96); Log Cabin (see page 94); Wrench (see page 100); Spider Web (see page 98); Album (see page 87); David and Goliath (see page 91); Interlocked Squares (see page 93); Whirlpool (see page 100); Missouri Daisy (see page 95); twelve ¼ x 3 inch joining strips vest fabric; six ¼ x 9¾ inch joining strips vest fabric; four ½ x 9¾ inch front contrast borders; two ½ x 18 inch back contrast borders; 6¾ x 18 inch vest fabric for back inset.

Diagram 3. Cut blocks, one each: Aunt Sukey's Choice (see page 87); Dresden Plate (see page 92); Variable Star (see page 99); Album (see page 87); Queen Charlotte's Crown (see page 97); Crazy Loons (see page 90); Wheel of Fortune (see page 99); North Star (see page 96); Crown of Thorns (see page 90); Little Star (see page 95); Cherry Basket (see page 89); Road to California (see page 98); two each ⅜ by 13½ inch vest front borders and front contrast borders; four ⅜ x 9¾ inch front contrast borders; two ⅜ x 9¾ inch vest borders; two ⅜ x 18 inch back contrast borders; one ⅜ x 18 inch vest border.

Diagram 4. Cut blocks, one each: Wood Lily (see page 100); Grandmother's Flower Garden (see page 92); Cornucopia (see page 89); Prairie Queen (see page 97); Grandmother's Fan (see page 92); House on a Hill (see page 93); four ⅞ x 3 inch contrast joining strips; four ⅜ x 10¾ inch contrast joining strips; 2 pattern C contrast fabric – ½ inch seam allowance included except where ¼ inch is indicated on lower edge; two 1¾ x 9½ inch front contrast border; one 1¾ x 18 inch back contrast border.

Diagram 5. Cut six Queen Charlotte's Crown blocks (see page 97); two ¾ x 3 inch contrast borders; four each ½ x 9¾ inch contrast borders and vest borders.

ASSEMBLY FOR ALL VESTS. Make blocks and sew together in rows as shown on diagrams. Sew borders together. Sew borders to blocks.

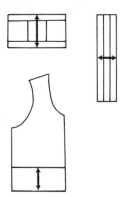

Measure width of completed block/border unit plus ½ inch for seam allowance on lower edge only. Measure vest from lower edge up to same measurement as your block/border unit and draw a seamline on wrong side of vest. Sew unit to vest with ¼ inch seam. Trim off excess vest fabric. Sew front vertical borders in the same way. (Vest diagram 4 has ½ inch seam allowance on front.)

With right sides together, sew vest back to front at shoulders. Repeat for lining.

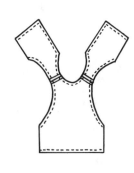

With right sides together, sew front seam of vest and lining. Place innerfacing on wrong side of vest. Stitch innerfacing with ¼ inch seam. Stitch vest and lining neck edge, front and back lower edges, armhole seams. Trim seams and clip curves. Turn to right side through shoulders.

Starting two inches above armhole seam and ending two inches below seam at lower edge, sew back to front at sides including lining in one continuous ½ inch seam. For vests with twelve block front/back border, use ¼ inch seam. Trim seam.

For vests with twelve block front/back border, pull unstitched section of blocks through opening in side seam. Sew front and back blocks together and finish sewing top of border unit to vest.

Turn under seam allowance on opening of lining and blindstitch (see page 14).

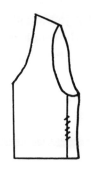

Four Points Handbag

Color Plate Page 52

SIZE. 16 x 16 inches.

MATERIALS. ⅛ yd. each colors B, C, D for blocks; ½ yd. color A for lining, blocks, pockets; ⅛ yd. color E for joining strips; ½ yd. color F for outside, casing; ½ yd. polyester fleece; two purse handles with 8 inch straight bottom.

CUTTING. Add ¼ inch seam allowance on all pieces. Cut eight Four Points blocks (see page 104); two 9 x 10 inch color A pockets; four 3 x 8½ inch color F casing; two 3 x 8½ inch polyester fleece casing; four 1 x 16 inch color E joining strip; two 1 x 16 inch color F outside; two 16 x 16 inch color A lining; two 16 x 16 inch polyester fleece; two 10 x 16 inch color F outside; pattern A; pattern B.

BLOCKS. Make eight Four Points blocks.

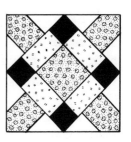

Sew blocks together in two rows with pattern B joining strips between, pattern A joining strips on each end, 1 x 16 inch joining strips on top and bottom.

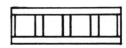

Sew 10 x 16 inch outside to lower edge of blocks and 1 x 16 inch outside to upper edge of blocks.

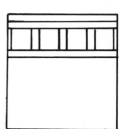

POCKET. With right sides together, stitch sides and one end. Trim corners and turn to right side.

Center pocket on lining with open edges even with lower edge of lining. Sew pocket to lining on sides.

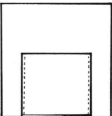

CASINGS. With right sides together, place two casings on polyester fleece. Sew the sides. Turn to right side and press. Repeat for other casing.

Fold each casing lengthwise over handle. Thread baste across bottom. Stitch ⅛ inch from raw edges.

ASSEMBLY. With right sides together, sew outside back to outside front on sides and bottom. Trim corners and turn to right side. Repeat for lining but do not turn to right side.

With wrong sides together, place lining in bag. Fold under ¼ inch around upper edge of outside and lining. Center casings on each side of bag. With lining slightly below outside fabric, thread baste together on upper edge and blindstitch or stitch close to edge using zipper foot.

BOX BOTTOM. Reach into bag and pull out together one corner of lining and outside. With lining side out, fold into a triangle. Stitch across base of triangle 1½ inches from point. Repeat for other corner.

End joining strip 4E   A

Joining strip 6E   B

Night and Noon Pillow

Color Plate Page 52

SIZE. 21 x 21 inches including ruffle.

MATERIAL. ⅔ yd. color A for blocks, ruffle; ⅛ yd. color B for blocks, borders; ⅛ yd. each colors C and D for blocks; ½ yd. color E for blocks, large triangles, back; 1½ yds. 5 or 6 oz. batting for stuffing or other desired stuffing material.

PATTERN. Enlarge traingle pattern A. Add ¼ inch seam allowance.

1 sq. = 2 in.
Add ¼ inch seam allowance

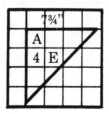

CUTTING. Add ¼ inch seam allowance on all pieces except where otherwise indicated. Cut nine Night and Noon blocks (see page 96); triangle pattern A; 16 x 16 inch color E back; two 1 x 9 inch color B borders; two 1 x 11 inch color B borders; three 6 x 44 inch color A ruffle—seam allowance included.

BLOCKS. Make nine Night and Noon blocks.

Sew the rows together.

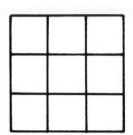

BORDERS. Sew a 1 x 9 inch border to each side of blocks. Sew 1 x 11 inch borders to remaining sides.

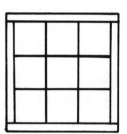

TRIANGLES. Sew pattern A triangles to borders.

RUFFLE. (See page 17).

STUFFING. (See page 19).

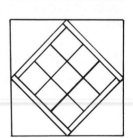

Christmas Ornaments

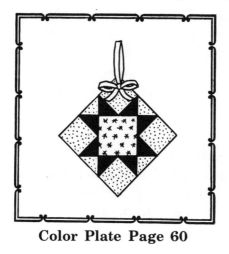

Color Plate Page 60

SIZE. 3 x 3 inches.

MATERIALS FOR 9 ORNAMENTS. ⅛ yd. solid red or green for back; 3 yds. (⅓ yd. each ornament) narrow red or green ribbon for bow and hanger; ⅛ yd. polyester fleece; assorted three inch quilt blocks made in Christmas colors. Recommended patterns are: Variable Star, Dresden Plate, Spider Web, Queen Charlotte's Crown, David and Goliath, Album (for writing name or date), North Star, Night and Noon, Missouri Daisy, Double T, Braced Star, Shooting Star, Interlocked Squares. (Try other patterns, too.)

CUTTING. Add ¼ inch seam allowance on all pieces. Quilt blocks made in Christmas colors; 3 x 3 inch red or green back (see page 104); 5 inch ribbon for hanger; 7 inch ribbon for bow.

EMBROIDERY. To embroider name or date on Album block, trace large Album name pattern piece onto a square of solid color fabric large enough to fit into an embroidery hoop. Thread baste around pattern line so it can be seen from right side of fabric. Write name or date within pattern lines and embroider with outline stitch (see page 15). Cut out pattern with ¼ inch seam allowance.

MAKE BLOCK.

ASSEMBLY. With right sides together, place top and back on polyester fleece. Sew together leaving a 2 inch opening in center of one side. Trim seams and corners. Turn to right side. Turn under seam allowance on opening and blindstitch (see page 14).

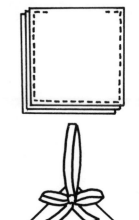

BOW AND HANGER. Tie a small bow. Fold 5 inch long ribbon hanger in half. Fold under ¼ inch on both ends and tack together. Sew hanger to corner of block. Sew ribbon to hanger.

Crazy Loons Album Cover

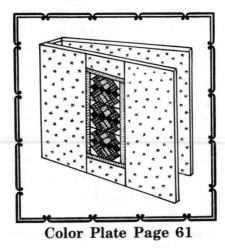

Color Plate Page 61

SIZE. Album must be 11 inches tall or over.

MEASURING.

1. One each, lining color A and polyester fleece. Measure album from front to back and top to bottom for finished width and length. Add 1 inch to width, 1 inch to length.

2. Four inside flaps color A. Measure from edge of cover to crease of spine for finished size. Add ¾ inch to width, 1 inch to length.

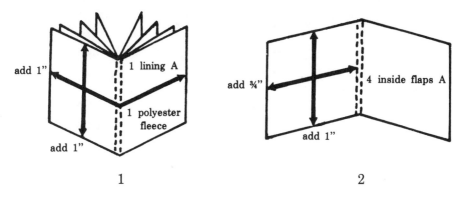

add 1" 1 lining A 1 polyester fleece add 1"

1

add ¾" 4 inside flaps A add 1"

2

3. One outside right extension color A. Measure from right edge of cover to beginning of spine. Subtract this width from width of block unit (4 in.) and divide by 2 for finished width of right cover extension. Add ¾ inch to width and 1 inch to length.

4. One each cover top and bottom extension color A. Subtract length of block unit (10 in.) from finished length of album (see 1). Divide by 2 for finished extension width. Add ¾ inch to length of each piece.

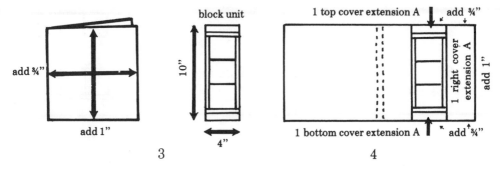

add ¾" add 1"

3

block unit 10" 4"

1 top cover extension A add ¾" 1 right cover extension A add 1" 1 bottom cover extension A add ¾"

4

5. One left-back cover extension color A. To find size of extension, add width of block unit (4 in.) to finished width of right extension (see 3). Subtract this sum from finished album width (see 1). Add ¾ inch to width and 1 inch to length.

¼ INCH SEAMS ALLOWED ON ALL PIECES.

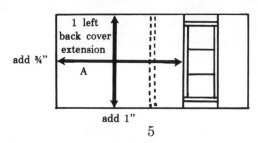

5

MATERIALS. Album; fabric color A for lining, inside flaps, blocks, cover extensions; ⅛ yd. each colors B, C for blocks, border, polyester fleece.

CUTTING. Add ¼ inch seam allowance on all pieces. Cut three Crazy Loon blocks (see **page 90**); **pattern A border; pattern B border;** lining; cover extensions; polyester fleece; inside flaps to your measurements.

BLOCKS. Make three Crazy Loon blocks.

Sew blocks together in a row.

BORDERS. Sew pattern B borders to blocks. Sew pattern A borders.

EXTENSIONS. Sew top and bottom cover extensions to blocks.

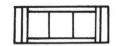

Sew right and left-back cover extensions to blocks.

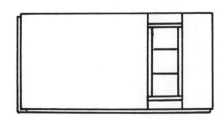

34

QUILTING (optional). Place cover on polyester fleece with right side up. For quilting, baste around block unit then quilt.

INSIDE FLAP. With right sides together, sew two inside flap pieces together on the side which will be placed along spine. Turn to right side and press. Repeat for other flap.

ASSEMBLY. Place flaps on right side of cover with raw edges together and matching seamlines. Thread baste.

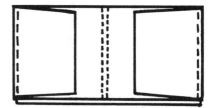

With right side together, place lining on flaps. Sew together, leaving an opening in center bottom for turning. Trim seams and corners. Turn to right side. Turn under seam allowance on opening and blindstitch (see page 14). Lightly press around edges.

A	Border 2C

B	Border 2C	fold

Two Little Soft Boxes

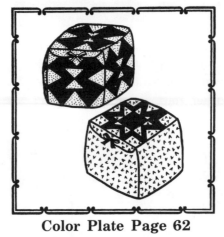

Color Plate Page 62

SIZE. 3 x 3 inches.

MATERIALS. ¼ yd. color A for Morning Star and Double Z blocks, Morning Star outside and tab outside, Double Z outside and tab outside; ¼ yd. color B for Morning Star and Double Z blocks, Double Z box lining and tab lining, Morning Star box lining and tab lining; ⅛ yd. heavy innerfacing; ⅛ yd. 5 or 6 oz. batting; ¼ yd. ⅛ inch wide ribbon to contrast with outside tab fabric; 11 x 13 inch chipboard or mounting board; rubber cement.

CUTTING. Add ¼ inch seam allowance on all patterns except where otherwise indicated. Morning Star Soft Box: Cut one Morning Star block (see page 102); five 3 x 3 inch color A outside (see page 104); six 3 x 3 inch color B lining; pattern A tab; pattern B chipboard and batting–seam allowance included. Double Z Soft Box: Cut five Double Z blocks (see page 102); six 3 x 3 inch color B lining (see page 104); one 3 x 3 inch color A outside; pattern A tab; pattern B chipboard and batting–seam allowance included.

BLOCKS. Make one Morning Star block or five Double Z blocks.

GLUE BATTING. With rubber cement, glue batting to both sides of all pattern B chipboard squares.

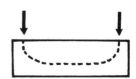

TAB. With right side up, place pattern A tab lining on tab innerfacing. With right sides together, place tab front on lining. Stitch, beginning and ending with vertical lines of stitching between end of pattern line and edge of fabric.

Trim seam to ⅛ inch and turn to right side. Press. Machine baste across opening ⅛ inch from edge. On lining side of tab, draw a new seamline 1⅛ inch from bottom edge.

ENVELOPES. Place two pins on seamline of one side of each outside and lining. Press under seam allowance at pin markers. Remove pins and open pressed seam allowance.

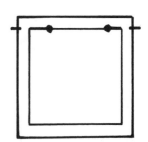

To make lid, place tab on lining with lining sides together. Place outside over tab. Pin baste matching seamlines of all three pieces. Stitch on three sides, beginning and ending at raw edge of unfolded pressed seam allowance. Trim seams and corners and turn to right side. Turn under pressed seam allowance at opening. Repeat for remaining envelopes (except for tab).

INSERT FILLER. Insert cardboard/batting into envelopes. Use a letter opener or nail file to gently push batting back into corners on all sides. Turn under seam allowance on opening and blindstitch (see page 14).

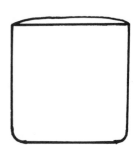

ASSEMBLY. Stitching from outside, blindstitch the four sides together, the bottom to sides, then the top (see page 14).

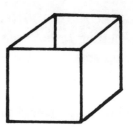

BOW. Make a tiny bow. Tack it to center of tab.

For each box: A
1A, 1B, 1 innerfacing

B

For each box:
12 batting
6 chipboard

Praire Queen Skirt Border

Color Plate Page 57

MATERIALS. Pattern and fabric for front wrap skirt; ⅛ yd. each of colors A, B, C, D for eight or nine blocks.

CUTTING. Add ¼ inch seam allowance on all pieces except where otherwise indicated. Cut quantity of 3 x 3 inch Prairie Queen blocks needed to fit between belt seamline and hemline (see page 97). Cut skirt as directed on pattern. Cut an extension of skirt fabric to match right skirt front 4¾ inches wide by length of skirt you have cut out–seam allowance included. Cut a 3½ x 3½ inch extension of skirt fabric for hem of block on lower edge of skirt–seam allowance included. Lengthen this extension if finished length of skirt does not divide evenly by three and more fabric is needed between bottom block and hemline.

BLOCKS. Make Prairie Queen blocks.

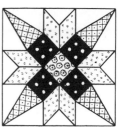

Sew blocks into a row.

39

BLOCK EXTENSION. Sew 3½ x 3½ inch lower edge skirt fabric extension to one end of row of blocks with ¼ inch seam.

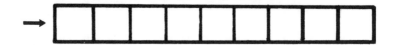

SKIRT EXTENSION. Cut off 1⅝ inch from right front of skirt–seam allowance included.

Sew 4¾ inch wide skirt fabric extension to right side of 1⅝ inch piece with ⅝ inch seam.

ATTACH BLOCKS. To prepare skirt for blocks, cut off 2¾ inch from right front of skirt–seam allowance included. Discard this piece.

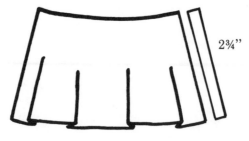

Matching seamline of top block to seamline of skirt top, sew blocks to skirt front with ¼ inch seam.

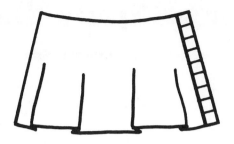

ATTACH EXTENSION. Matching seamline of top block to seamline of narrow part of extension, sew other side of blocks to extension with ¼ inch seam.

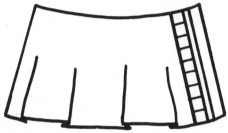

HEM EXTENSION. Press wide part of extension to inside of skirt on seamline. Press under ¼ inch on long edge and slipstitch to seam leaving 7 inches unstitched at lower edge until after hemming. Finish skirt following directions on pattern.

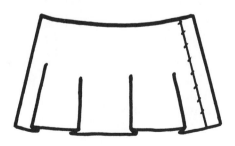

Bachelor's Puzzle Doll Quilt

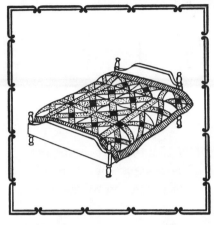

Color Plate Page 55

SIZE. 7 x 7 inches.

MATERIALS. ¼ yd. color A for blocks; ⅛ yd. each colors B and C for blocks; ¼ yd. color D for borders, back; ¼ yd. white flannel for filler.

CUTTING. Add ¼ inch seam allowance on all pieces. Cut four Bachelor's Puzzle blocks (see page 88); pattern A border; pattern B border (see page 88); 7 x 7 inch flannel; 7 x 7 inch color D back.

BLOCKS. Make four Bachelor's Puzzle blocks.

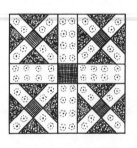

Sew blocks together. Sew rows together.

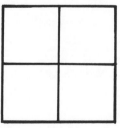

BORDER. Sew pattern A borders to each side of blocks. Sew pattern B borders.

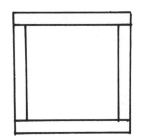

ASSEMBLY. With right sides together, place top and back on flannel. Sew together leaving a 3 inch opening in center of one side for turning. Trim seams and corners. Turn to right side. Turn under seam allowance on opening and blindstitch (see page 14).

Braced Star Doll Quilt

SIZE. 3½ x 6½ inches.

MATERIALS. ⅛ yd. color A for blocks, border; ⅛ yd. color B for blocks, back; ⅛ yd. white flannel for filler.

CUTTING. Add ¼ inch seam allowance on all pieces. Cut two Braced Star blocks (see page 103); pattern A border; pattern B border; pattern C back and flannel.

BLOCKS. Make two Braced Star blocks.

Sew blocks together.

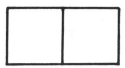

BORDER AND ASSEMBLY. (See Border and Assembly, Bachelor's Puzzle Doll Quilt.)

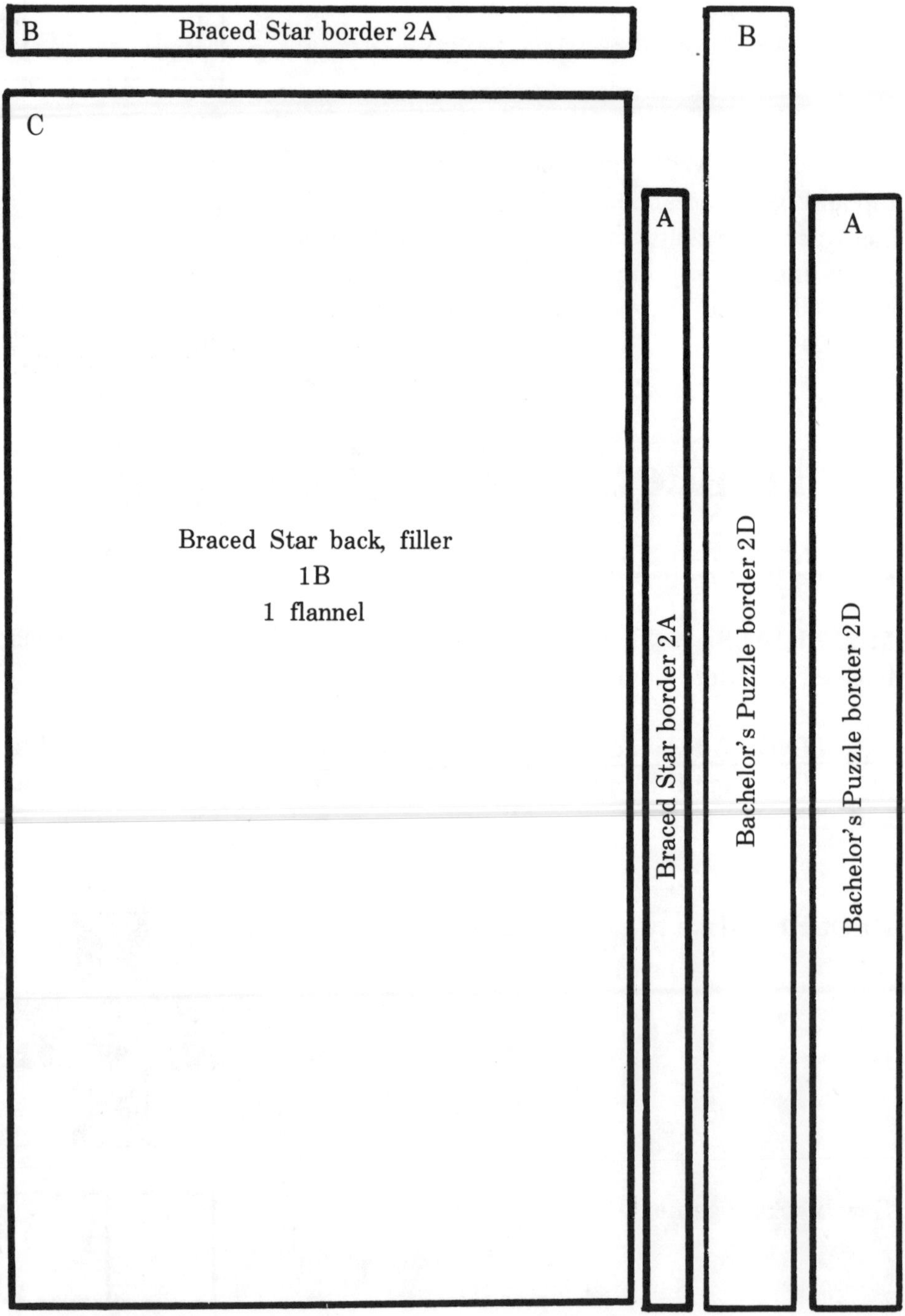

B   Braced Star border 2A

C

Braced Star back, filler
1B
1 flannel

B

A

A

Braced Star border 2A

Bachelor's Puzzle border 2D

Bachelor's Puzzle border 2D

Shooting Star Doll Quilt

SIZE. 13 x 22 inches.

MATERIALS. ⅜ yd. color A for blocks, inner border; ½ yd. color B for blocks, back; ¼ yd. color C for blocks, outer border, ⅜ yd. polyester fleece.

CUTTING. Add ¼ inch seam allowance on all pieces. Cut eighteen Shooting Star blocks (see page 103); two 1 x 11 inch color A inner borders; two 1 x 18 inch color A inner borders; two 1 x 13 inch color C outer borders; two 1 x 20 inch color C outer borders; 3 x 22 inch color B back; 3 x 22 inch polyester fleece.

BLOCKS. Make eighteen Shooting Star blocks.

Sew blocks together. Sew rows together.

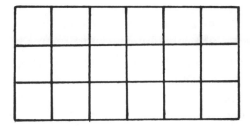

BORDERS. Sew 1 x 18 inch inner borders to each side of blocks. Sew 1 x 11 inch inner borders to top and bottom of blocks. Sew 1 x 20 inch outer borders to each side border. Sew 1 x 18 inch outer top and bottom borders.

ASSEMBLY. (See Assembly, Bachelor's Puzzle Doll Quilt.)

45

Interlocked Squares Placemats

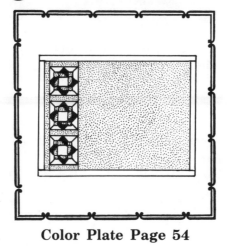

Color Plate Page 54

SIZE. 12 x 17 inches.

MATERIALS FOR SET OF FOUR. ⅛ yd. color A for blocks; 1⅜ yds. color B for back, front, joining strips; ½ yd. color C for blocks, binding; ¾ yd. polyester fleece.

CUTTING. Add ¼ inch seam allowance on all pieces except where otherwise indicated. Cut twelve Interlocked Squares blocks (see page 93); pattern A; pattern B; four 1 x 12 inch color B border; eight 2 x 12 inch color C binding; eight 2 x 18 inch color C binding; four 12 x 17 inch color B back; four 12 x 13 inch color B front; four 12 x 17 inch polyester fleece—seam allowance included.

BLOCKS. Make twelve Interlocked Squares blocks.

Sew three blocks together with pattern A joining strip between and pattern B joining strip on top and bottom.

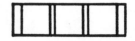

46

Sew border to left side of blocks.
Sew front to right side of blocks.

QUILTING (optional). With right side up, place front on polyester fleece. For quilting, baste around blocks then quilt.

ASSEMBLY. Place front on wrong side of back. Baste around edges.

BINDING. Press under ¼ inch on one long edge of each strip of binding. With right sides of front and 12 inch long binding together, sew binding to each side of placemat. Turn binding to back and blindstitch (see page 14). Repeat for 18 inch long binding on top and bottom of placemat and blindstitch across binding ends.

A
Joining strip 8B

B
Top and bottom joining strip 8B

Grandmother's Fan Jacket

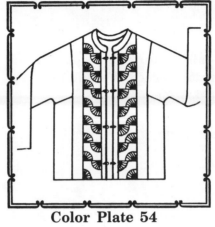

Color Plate 54

MATERIALS. Jacket pattern and fabric for jacket (I used prequilted muslin); ⅛ yd. each colors A, B, C, D, E, F prints for blocks; ⅛ yd. solid color G for blocks (use one of these fabrics for jacket lining); 4 frog closures; ⅛ yd. polyester fleece (if using quilted fabric for jacket); ¼ yd. solid color fabric for applique backing (I used unquilted muslin to match jacket). *Note:* Some jacket patterns may require more blocks.

CUTTING. Add ¼ inch seam allowance on all pieces except where otherwise indicated. Cut fifteen Grandmother's Fan blocks (see page 92), sixteen applique backing for fans (see page 104); jacket and lining according to your pattern; two 3¼ x 24 inch polyester fleece—seam allowance included.

BLOCKS. Make Fourteen Grandmother's Fan blocks.

Make two blocks with just one fan.

Sew together seven blocks and one fan block for each row.

ASSEMBLY. Cut off a 1⅞ inch piece from each side of jacket front–¼ inch seam allowance included on inside patchwork edge, ⅝ inch seam allowance included on outside neck and bottom edges. Save these pieces.

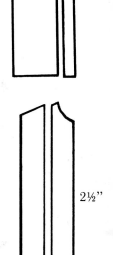

1⅞"

Cut off another 2½ inch piece from each jacket front. Discard these pieces.

2½"

Matching seamline of bottom block to jacket seamline, sew a row of blocks to each jacket front with ¼ inch seam. Press. Place jacket front pattern on each jacket front and cut off excess of half blocks on neck edge according to pattern.

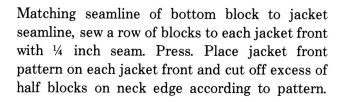
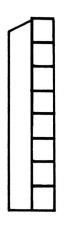

Sew a 1⅞ inch piece of jacket fabric to other side of each row of blocks with ¼ inch seam. Press.

If using quilted jacket fabric, place the strip of polyester fleece on wrong side of each row of blocks. Slipstitch over seams.

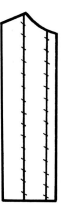

FINISHING. Follow directions on pattern for finishing jacket.

Three Petite Pin Cushions

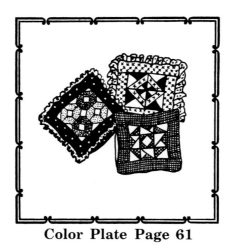

Color Plate Page 61

SIZE. 5 x 5 inches.

MATERIALS. ¼ yd. color A for block, border, back; ⅛ yd. each colors B and C; ⅔ yd. ½ or ¾ inch wide gathered eyelet or lace for each pin cushion; unbonded batting for stuffing.

CUTTING. Add ¼ inch seam allowance on all pieces. Cut one Kansas Dugout, Criss Cross, Air Castle (see page 101); pattern A and B borders; pattern C back.

BLOCK. Make Blocks.

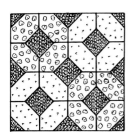 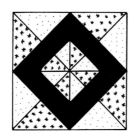 

(above) Road to California patchwork blocks in shades of peach form a pretty crisscross design (left). Pastel Night and Noon blocks create a lovely focal point (right). (below) Four Points quilt blocks embellish this charming handbag.

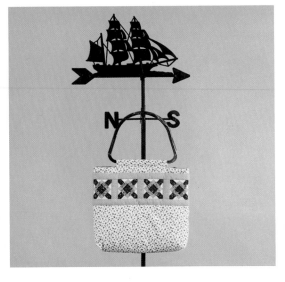

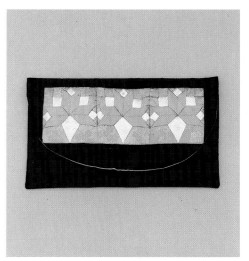

(above left) An elegant satin and taffeta clutch is inset with Cornucopia miniatures. (above right) An inset of Queen Charlotte's Crown patchwork makes a pretty trim for a sundress. Modeled by Becky Mlekush. (below) Miniature Wrench blocks adorn the border of this appliqued baby quilt.

(above) Rainbows of Grandmother's Fan miniatures cascade down the front of this beautiful jacket. Modeled by Dawna-Dale Williams. (below) Interlocked Squares placemats add the charm of patchwork to a table setting.

(above) Dainty Missouri Daisy blocks are repeated around the front and back of this exquisite vest. Modeled by Dawn Wright. (below left) This Bachelor's Puzzle doll bed quilt will set the decorating theme for a miniature bedroom. (below right) A row of assorted patchwork blocks trims this distinctive handbag.

A spectacular array of thirty miniature quilt blocks produced this delightful
sampler wall quilt.

(above) The edge of a front wrap skirt becomes a showplace of colorful Prairie Queen patchwork. Modeled by Liz Oritz. (below left) Missouri Daisy patchwork pockets add an interesting highlight to this jumper. Modeled by Shelley Williams. (below right) A casual Cornucopia clutch makes a useful and unique accessory.

(above) Blue jeans and corduroys have been recycled into sturdy and attractive Wrench potholders.

(above) A border of miniature patchwork completes this charming pinafore made by Barbara Breen and modeled by Heather Breen. (left) Queen Charlotte's Crown blocks have been quarter turned to achieve an attractive border design. Shown with matching handbag. Modeled by Mary Hoge.

(above) The double row arrangement of twelve miniatures produces a striking vest trim. Modeled by Annie Toy. (below) A bright row of tri-colored Chevron blocks makes a novel curtain border.

(above left) Miniature patchwork ornaments add a special festive spirit to this enchanting Christmas tree. (below right) A Chevron border was designed to add a unique band of color to this casual blouse. Modeled by Sheri Lopez.

(above) Night and Noon
(below) Cherry Basket

60

(above left) Pretty three inch quilt blocks are the perfect size for pin cushions. (above right) This album with Crazy Loons patchwork has become a prized family keepsake. (below) Six vertical miniature blocks combine to make an eyecatching vest front. Made and modeled by Nancy Donahue.

(above) Intricate patchwork blocks have created a stunning vest edging. Modeled by Sharon Roman. (below left) Soft boxes decorated with miniatures are appealing storage places for small treasures.

BORDER. Sew pattern A border to block. Sew pattern B border.

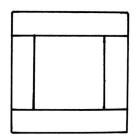

LACE TRIM. Starting in center of one side of block, with right sides together, turn under ¼ inch of lace. Pin baste lace to block adding a little extra fullness in corners and overlap ¼ inch at other end where lace meets. Stitch.

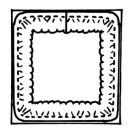

ASSEMBLY. With right sides together, sew back to top leaving a two inch opening in center of one side for turning. Trim seams and corners. Turn to right side.

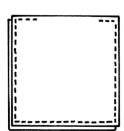

STUFF. With unbonded batting, stuff pin cushion. Turn under seam allowance on opening and blindstitch (see page 14).

B

Border
For each pin cushion 2A

A

Border
For each pin cushion 2A

C

Back
For each pin cushion 1A

Miniature Sampler Wall Quilt

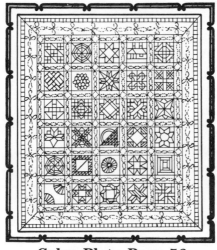

Color Plate Page 56

SIZE. 27¼ x 31¼ inches.

MATERIALS. ⅜ yd. each of six fabrics for blocks, patchwork border; ⅛ yd. color A for joining squares; 1⅛ yds. color B for joining strips, back, borders, rod pocket; 1 yd. batting.

CUTTING. Add ¼ inch seam allowance on all pieces except where otherwise indicated. Cut 30 blocks (see pages 87 to 100); 71 pattern A joining strips; 42 pattern B joining squares; 132 pattern C border patchwork; two ⅝ x 27¼ inch color B borders; two ⅝ x 31¼ inch color B borders; two 2 x 27¼ inch color B borders; two 2 x 31¼ inch color B borders; 33 x 33 inch color B back; 33 x 33 inch batting; 5 x 28 inch color B rod pocket–seam allowance included.

BLOCKS. Make 30 blocks.

SEW ROWS. Sew horizontal rows of blocks together with a pattern A joining strip between each block and on both ends of row.

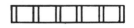

row 1: Road to California, Spider Web, Variable Star, House on a Hill, David and Goliath.

row 2: Crazy Loons, Grandmother's Flower Garden, Prairie Queen, Whirlpool, Bachelor's Puzzle.

row 3: Wrench, Aunt Sukey's Choice, Crown of Thorns, Album, Little Star.

row 4: Cornucopia, Wood Lily, Cherry Basket, Night and Noon, Missouri Daisy.

row 5: Wheel of Fortune, Lady of the Lake, Dresden Plate, North Star, Log Cabin.

row 6: Grandmother's Fan, Double T, Interlocked Squares, Queen Charlotte's Crown, Broad Arrows.

JOINING BANDS. Sew six pattern B joining squares together with a joining strip between each square.

ASSEMBLE ROWS. Sew a joining band to top of each row of blocks and to bottom of row 6.

Sew all rows together.

PATCHWORK BORDER. Sew two rows of 31 pattern C pieces and two rows of 35 pattern C pieces.

ASSEMBLE BORDER. Sew a ⅝ x 27¼ inch border to each 31 piece row and a ⅝ x 31¼ inch border to each 35 piece row.

Sew a 2 x 27¼ inch border to each 31 piece row and a 2 x 31¼ inch border to each 35 piece row.

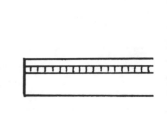

ATTACH BORDER. Sew side borders to quilt top ending stitching at corner seamline. Sew top and bottom borders the same way.

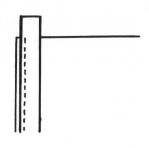

To miter corners, place pattern D mitering triangle even with seamline on outer border and on corner of inner border. Draw a seamline down long edge of triangle. Repeat for all corners. Sew miters and trim seam.

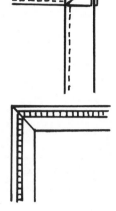

MARK FOR QUILTING. Mark quilting design E on joining squares, design F on joining strips, design G on widest color B border.

QUILT ASSEMBLY. With right sides together, place top and back on batting. Stitch together leaving a twelve inch opening in center bottom for turning. Trim seams and corners. Turn to right side. Turn under seam allowance on opening and blindstitch (see page 14). Lightly press edges of quilt.

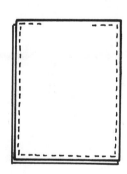

QUILTING. Baste for quilting.

Cut two 6 x 34 inch strips of scrap fabric. Baste strips to edge of quilt to hold hoop for quilting near edge. Quilt.

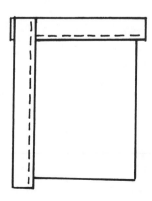

ROD POCKET. With right sides together, fold rod pocket in half lengthwise. Stitch long edge with ¼ inch seam. Turn to right side and press. Press under ½ inch on each end. Blindstitch rod pocket to back ½ inch from top edge.

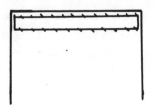

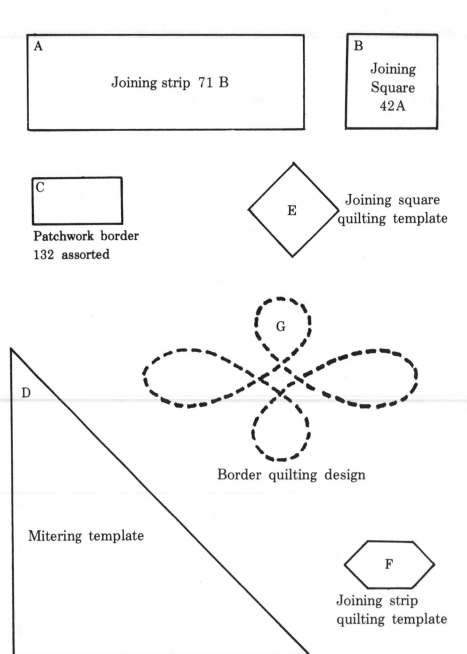

A

Joining strip 71 B

B

Joining
Square
42A

C

Patchwork border
132 assorted

E

Joining square
quilting template

G

Border quilting design

D

Mitering template

F

Joining strip
quilting template

Wrench Potholders

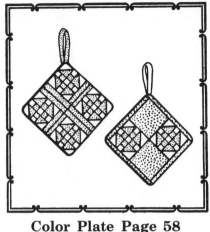

Color Plate Page 58

SIZE. 7 x 7 inches.

MATERIALS. ¼ yd. color A for blocks and back; ⅛ yd. color B for blocks; ¼ yd. terry cloth for filler.

CUTTING. Add ¼ inch seam allowance on all pieces. Two Wrench Potholder: Cut two Wrench blocks (see page 100); pattern A hanger; pattern B and C borders; 7 x 7 inch color A back; one or two 7 x 7 inch terry cloth; 3 x 3 inch color A (see page 100); Four Wrench potholder: Cut four Wrench blocks; pattern A hanger; pattern D joining strips; 7 x 7 inch color A back; one or two 7 x 7 inch terry cloth.

TWO WRENCH POTHOLDER

BLOCKS. Make two Wrench blocks.

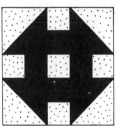

Sew a solid color block to each Wrench block.

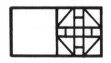

Sew the rows together.

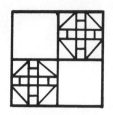

BORDERS. Sew pattern B borders then pattern C borders.

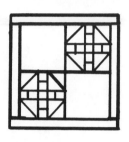

HANGER. To make hanger, pattern A, press under ⅛ inch on each long edge. Press hanger in half lengthwise. Stitch close to edge.

Place hanger diagonally in one corner on front of potholder with raw edges even. Thread baste end of hanger to front.

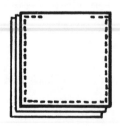

ASSEMBLY. Place front on terry cloth with right side up. With right sides together, place back on front. Sew together leaving a 4 inch opening in the center of one side. Turn under seam allowance on opening and blindstitch (see page 14).

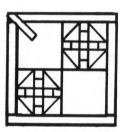

FOUR WRENCH POTHOLDER

BLOCKS. Make four Wrench blocks.

70

JOINING STRIPS. Sew a pattern D joining strip to one side of each block.

Sew another joining strip to each block as shown.

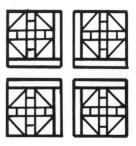

Sew rows together.

HANGER AND ASSEMBLY. (See Two Wrench, Potholder Hanger and Assembly.)

D	
	Joining strip 8 A

B		fold
	Border 2 A	

C		fold
	Border 2 A	

A	
	Hanger
	Two Wrench potholder 1 B
	Four Wrench potholder 1 A

Road To California Pillow

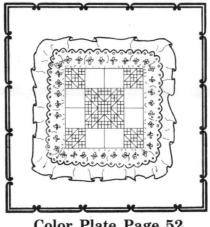

Color Plate Page 52

SIZE. 18 x 18 inches including ruffle.

MATERIALS. 1 yd. color A for back, ruffle, blocks; 1½ yds. two inch wide gathered eyelet; ⅛ yd. solid color for pillow top; ⅛ yd. each colors B, C, D for blocks; 1½ yds. 5 or 6 oz. batting for stuffing or other desired stuffing material.

CUTTING. Add ¼ inch seam allowance on all pieces except where otherwise indicated. Cut 12 x 12 inch color A back; two 7 x 44 inch color A ruffle—seam allowance included; eight Road to California blocks (see page 98); eight 3 x 3 inch solid color (see page 104).

BLOCKS. Make eight Road to California blocks.

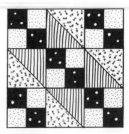

Sew horizontal rows. Sew all rows together.

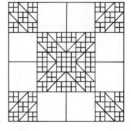

RUFFLES. (See page 18.)

STUFFING. (See page 19.)

Teddy Bear Baby Quilt

Color Plate Page 53

SIZE. 29 x 29 inches.

MATERIALS. ¼ yd. color A for blocks; ¼ yd. color B for blocks, paws, ears; 1⅔ yds. color C for applique backing, back; ⅔ yd. color D for teddy bear, borders, joining strips; ⅛ yd. color E for nose; crib size batting; embroidery thread to contrast with colors B and C.

PATTERN. Enlarge teddy bear pattern F. Add ¼ inch seam allowance.

1 sq. = 1 in.
Add ¼ inch seam allowance

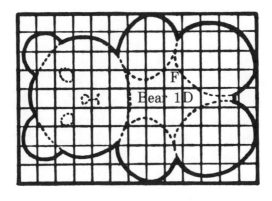

CUTTING. Add ¼ inch seam allowance on all pieces except where otherwise indicated. Cut patterns A, B, C, D, E, F; twenty four Wrench blocks (see page 100); two 1 x 19 inch color D borders; two 1 x 21 inch color D borders; two 1 x 27 inch color D borders; two 1 x 29 inch color D borders; 19 x 19 inch color C applique backing; 35 x 35 inch color C back; 35 x 35 inch batting–seam allowance included.

APPLIQUE. Applique teddy bear to applique backing.

EMBROIDERY. Embroider nose with satin stitch, mouth with outline stitch and running stitches for areas shown with broken lines (see page 15).

BORDERS. Sew 1 x 19 inch borders to sides of applique backing. Sew 1 x 21 inch top and bottom borders.

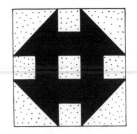

BLOCKS. Make twenty four Wrench blocks.

JOINING BLOCKS. Sew two rows of five Wrench blocks together with pattern A joining strip between each block and on top and bottom of row. Sew two rows of seven Wrench blocks with a joining strip between each block.

Sew a row of five blocks to each side border. Sew rows of seven blocks to top and bottom borders.

BORDERS. Sew 1 x 27 inch side borders to blocks. Sew 1 x 29 inch top and bottom borders.

BASTE FOR QUILTING. Mark quilting design. Place batting on wrong side of back. Center top on batting with right side up. Baste then quilt.

BINDING. Cut off excess batting to raw edge of top on all sides. Cut off excess back leaving 1 inch remaining for binding. Turn under ½ inch of back and fold over to top and blindstitch (see page 14).

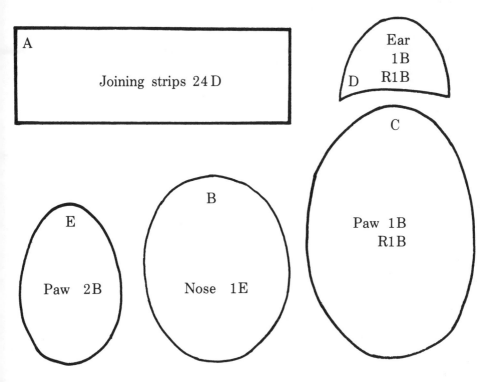

A

Joining strips 24 D

Ear
1 B
D   R1B

C

Paw 1B
R1B

B

E

Paw 2B

Nose 1E

Cornucopia Clutch

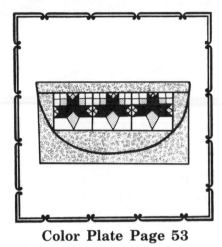

Color Plate Page 53

SIZE. 6 x 11 inches.

MATERIALS. ⅛ yd. each of colors A, B, C for blocks; ⅓ yd. color D for bag front, inside bottom; ⅓ yd. color E for lining, inside bottom lining; ⅓ yd. polyester fleece; 1 Velcro snap to match bag front fabric.

PATTERN. Enlarge patterns A and B. Add ¼ inch seam allowance.

1 sq. = 2 in.
Add ¼ inch seam allowance

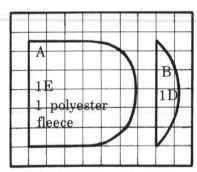

CUTTING. Add ¼ inch seam allowance on all pieces. Cut pattern A lining and polyester fleece; patterns B and C bag front patchwork; three Cornucopia blocks (see page 89); two 6 x 11 inch color D bag front and inside bottom front; 6 x 11 inch color E inside bottom lining; 1 x 11 inch color D bag front patchwork.

BLOCKS. Make three cornucopia blocks.

Sew blocks together in a row.

PATCHWORK FRONT FLAP. Sew one pattern C piece onto each end of row of blocks. Sew 1 x 11 inch piece to top of blocks and pattern B piece to bottom.

Sew patchwork to bag front.

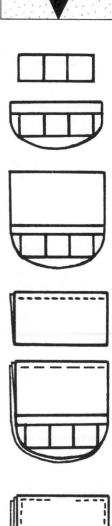

INSIDE BOTTOM. With right sides together, sew 6 x 11 inch bag front and lining across one end. Turn to right side and press.

ASSEMBLY. Place bag top on pattern A polyester fleece with right side up. Place inside bottom on bag top with color D sides together, matching seamlines. Thread baste.

With right side down, place pattern A lining on inside bottom. Sew together leaving a 4½ inch opening for turning in center of bag bottom. Trim seams and corners, clip curves. Turn bag and inside bottom to right side. Turn under seam allowance on opening and blindstitch (see page 14). Press edges.

TOP STITCH. Top stitch seam on bag front. Blindstitch Velcro snaps to lining side of flap and to bag front.

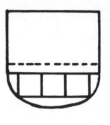

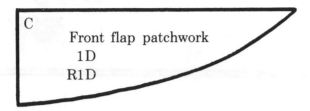

$\mathscr{M}$issouri $\mathscr{D}$aisy Pockets

Color Plate Page 57

SIZE. 4 x 4 inches.

MATERIALS. Dress or jumper; ⅛ yd. each colors A and B for blocks; ⅛ yd. color C for lining, borders.

CUTTING. Add ¼ inch seam allowance on all pieces. Cut two Missouri Daisy blocks using only two colors (see page 95); patterns A and B borders; pattern C lining.

BLOCKS. Make two Missouri Daisy blocks.

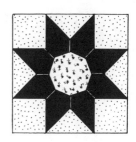

BORDERS. Sew pattern A top and bottom borders to each block. Sew pattern B side borders.

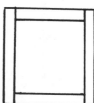

LINING. With right sides together, sew pattern C lining to block leaving a 2 inch opening in center bottom for turning. Trim seams and corners. Turn to right side. Press under seam allowance on opening.

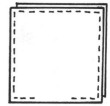

ATTACH. With open edges at lower edge of pocket, sew pockets to dress.

A
Border 2 C

B
Border 2 C

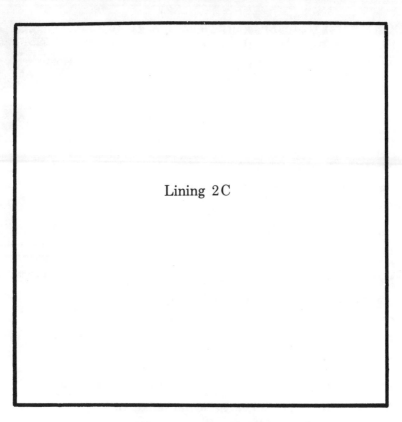

Lining 2 C

Sundress

Color Plate Page 53

SIZE. 10.

MATERIALS. 2¾ yds. for sundress and facing; ⅛ yd. each colors A, B, C for blocks.

PATTERN. Enlarge pattern–⅝ inch seam allowance included except where otherwise indicated.

1 sq. = 3 in.

⅝ inch seam allowance included except where otherwise indicated.

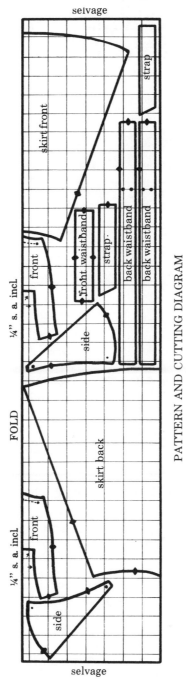

PATTERN AND CUTTING DIAGRAM

CUTTING. Add ¼ inch seam allowance on blocks. Cut two Queen Charlotte's Crown blocks (see page 97); sundress (cutting layout see page 97) – ⅝ inch seam allowance included except where otherwise indicated.

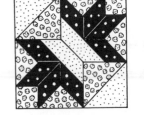

BLOCKS. Make two Queen Charlotte's Crown blocks and sew them together.

PATCHWORK INSET. Staystitch ¼ inch from edge around front neck inset area. Clip corners to stay stitching. Sew blocks to front with ¼ inch seam.

STRAPS. With right sides together, sew straps to front. Repeat for front facing.

SIDES. With right sides together, sew long unnotched edge of sides. Turn to right side and press.

TOP ASSEMBLY. With right sides together, stitch sides to front.

Sew facing to front from one side around straps, neck, to other side using ¼ inch seam allowance only around neck edge. Press. Turn under seam allowance on facing and hem over seam.

Sew back waistband to front waistband leaving right side open between circles at side seam. Press seams open. Repeat for waistband facing.

With right sides together, pin waistband to top matching notches and large circles. Adjust gathers to fit. Stitch.

Pin right side of facing to wrong side of bodice. Stitch around waistband ending at large circles. Clip to stitching at large circles. Trim seams and corners and turn waistband to right side. Press.

SKIRT. With right sides together, sew skirt back to front at side seams. On back edges, turn under narrow hem and stitch.

ASSEMBLY. With right sides together, sew skirt to waistband matching seams. Trim seams and press toward waistband. Turn under seam allowance on facing and hem over seam.

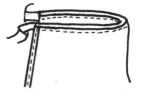

Pin straps to back and adjust to fit. Stitch close to upper edge of waistband. Hem.

Curtain With Chevron Border

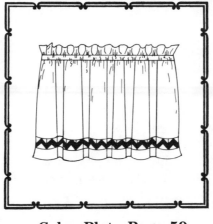

Color Plate Page 59

MEASURING FOR LENGTH. Measure length of window. Add 6 inches for casing and top gathers. Add 9½ inches for hem and lining for blocks—seam allowance included. (Curtain extends 2¾ inches above window and 3 inches below window.)

MEASURING FOR WIDTH. Measure width of window. Add 4½ inches for hems—seam allowance included. (Curtain extends 1 inch beyond window on each side.) Double this total for fabric for width.

3 x 3 INCH BLOCKS. For amount of blocks required, divide width of window by three. If there is a remainder, an extension will be added to blocks in that amount.

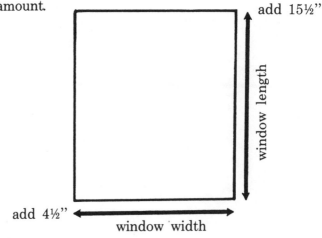

add 15½"

window length

add 4½"

window width

CUTTING. Add ¼ inch seam allowance on all pieces. Cut Chevron blocks as needed (see page 104).

BLOCKS. Make Chevron blocks.

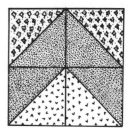

Sew blocks together in a row.

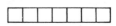

EXTENSION. If your window width **divides by three evenly,** cut two pieces of curtain fabric 1½ x 3½ inches–seam allowance included. Sew one of the extensions to each end of row of blocks with ¼ inch seam.

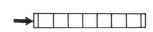

If your window width did not divide by three evenly, divide the remainder by two and add 1½ inches for the width of each extension. Cut two pieces of curtain fabric this width by 3½ inches– seam allowance included. Sew one extension to each end of row of blocks with ¼ inch seam.

ATTACH BLOCKS. To prepare curtain for blocks, cut off 9½ inches from lower edge of curtain. Then cut off 2½ inches from lower edge of upper section of curtain–seam allowance included. Discard the 2½ inch piece.

upper curtain section

2½"

9½"
lower curtain section

Sew blocks to upper section of curtain and to 9½ inch lower section with ¼ inch seam.

HEMS. For bottom hem and block lining, press under ¼ inch on lower edge of curtain then press under another 6 inches and slipstitch to block seam.

For side hems, press under ¼ inch on each side of curtain. Press under a one inch hem. Stitch.

For top hem, press under ¼ inch on upper edge of curtain then press under another 2¾ inches. Stitch. For casing, measure 1½ inches up from previous hem stitching and stitch.

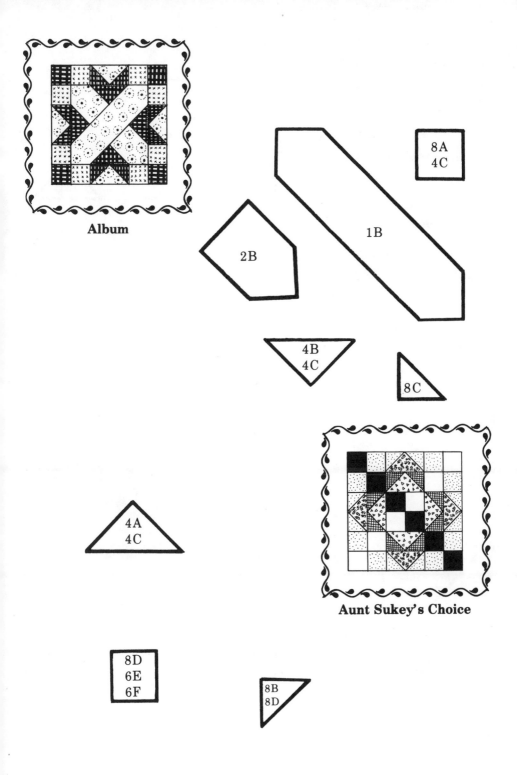

Album

8A
4C

1B

2B

4B
4C

8C

4A
4C

Aunt Sukey's Choice

8D
6E
6F

8B
8D

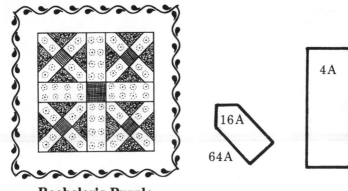

Bachelor's Puzzle

The doll quilt cutting instructions are beside each piece

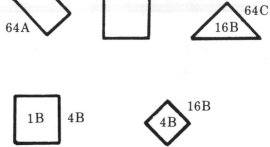

16A
64A

4A   16A

64C
16B

1B   4B

16B
4B

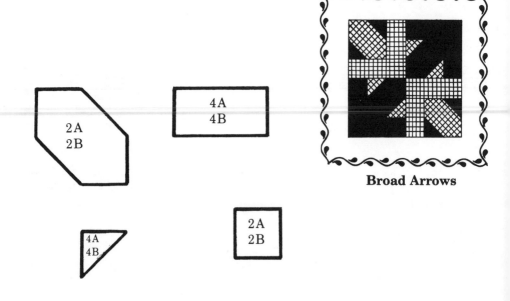

2A
2B

4A
4B

4A
4B

2A
2B

Broad Arrows

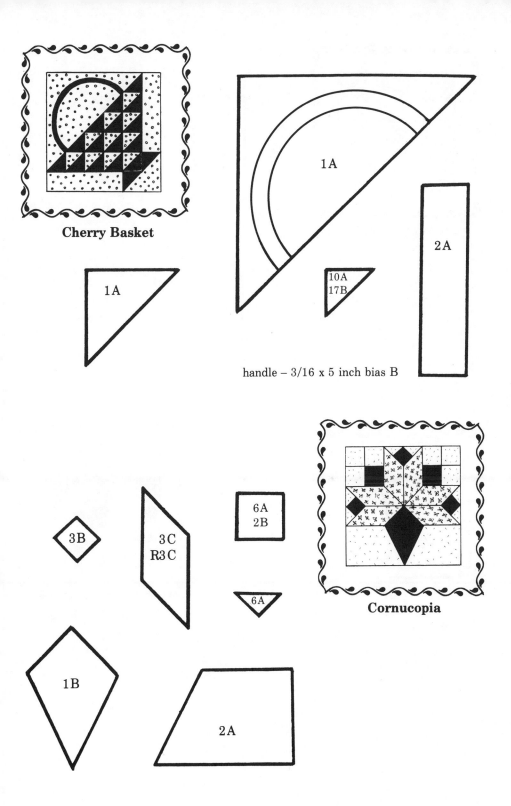

Cherry Basket

1A

1A

10A
17B

2A

handle – 3/16 x 5 inch bias B

3B

3C
R3C

6A
2B

6A

Cornucopia

1B

2A

89

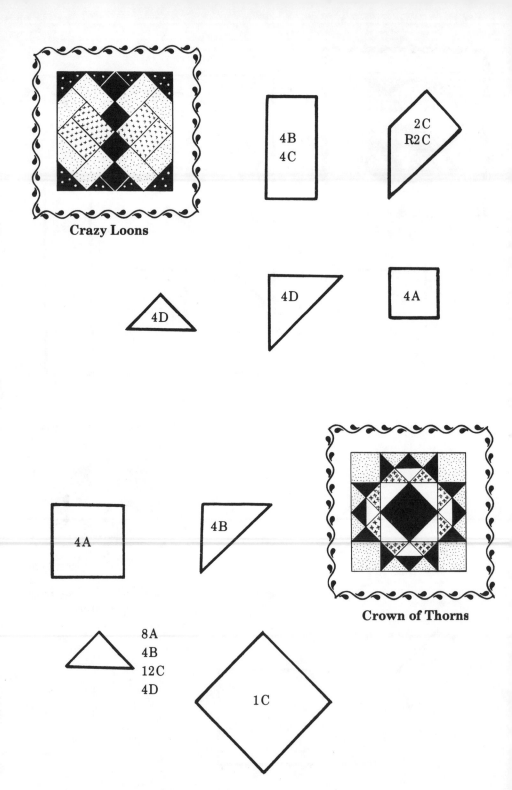

Crazy Loons

4B
4C

2C
R2C

4D

4D

4A

4A

4B

Crown of Thorns

8A
4B
12C
4D

1C

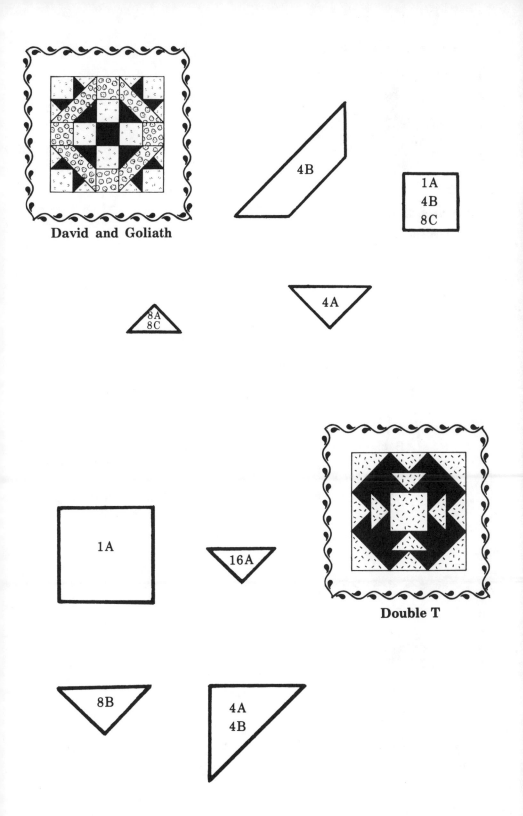

David and Goliath

4B

1A
4B
8C

4A

8A
8C

1A

16A

Double T

8B

4A
4B

91

4A
4B
4C
4D

Dresden Plate

1E

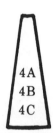

4A
4B
4C

2D

Grandmother's Fan

Grandmother's Flower Garden

1A
6B
12C

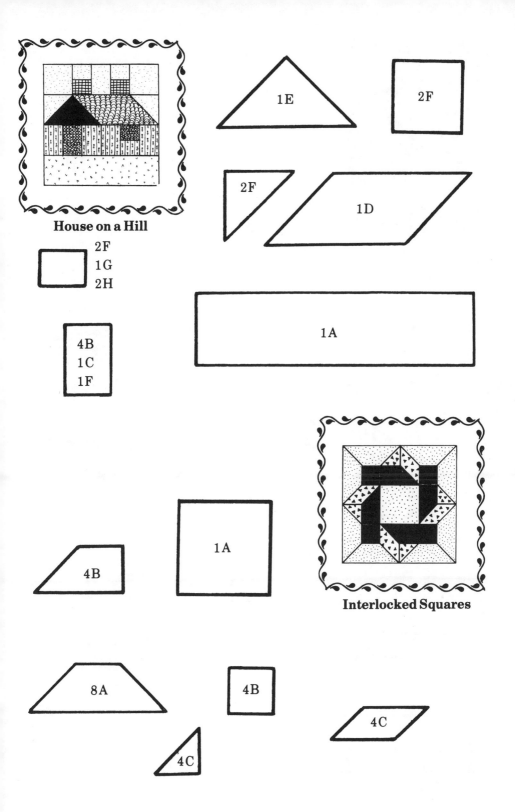

House on a Hill

1E

2F

2F

1D

2F
1G
2H

1A

4B
1C
1F

1A

4B

Interlocked Squares

8A

4B

4C

4C

Lady of the Lake

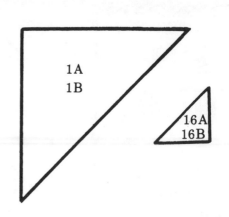

1A
1B

16A
16B

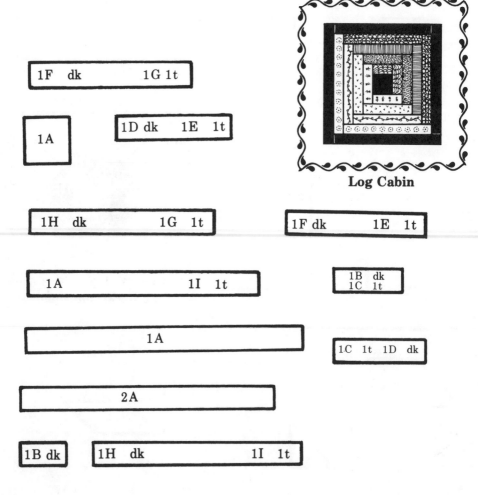

1F   dk   1G 1t

1A

1D dk   1E   1t

Log Cabin

1H   dk   1G   1t

1F dk   1E   1t

1A   1I   1t

1B   dk
1C   1t

1A

1C   1t   1D   dk

2A

1B dk   1H   dk   1I   1t

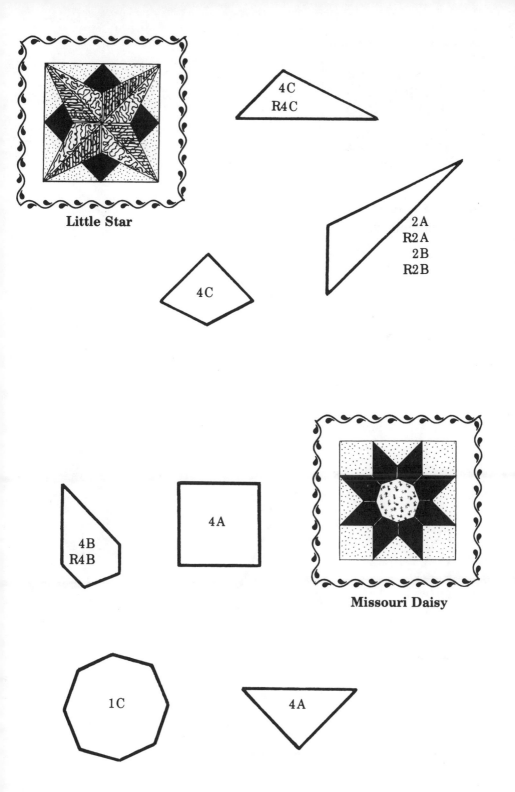

Little Star

4C
R4C

2A
R2A
2B
R2B

4C

Missouri Daisy

4B
R4B

4A

1C

4A

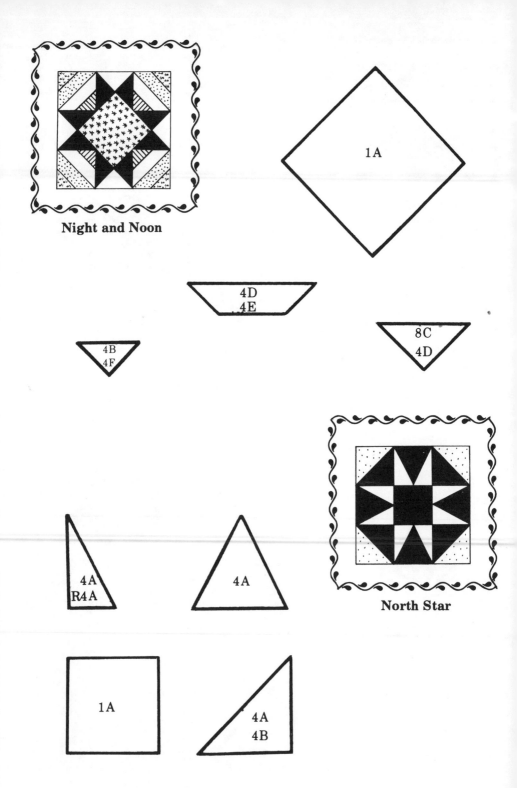

Night and Noon

1A

4D
4E

8C
4D

4B
4F

North Star

4A
R4A

4A

1A

4A
4B

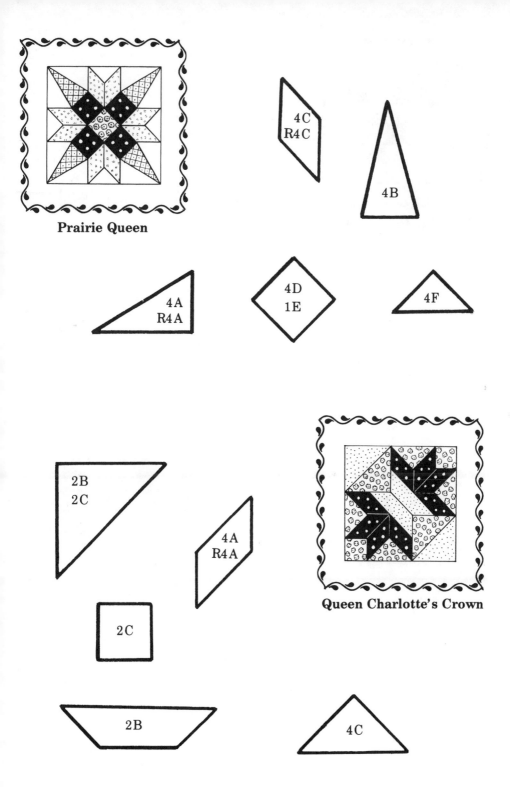

Prairie Queen

4C
R4C

4B

4A
R4A

4D
1E

4F

2B
2C

4A
R4A

Queen Charlotte's Crown

2C

2B

4C

Road to California

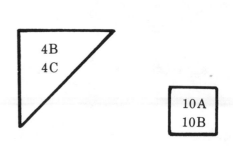

4B
4C

10A
10B

4C
R4C

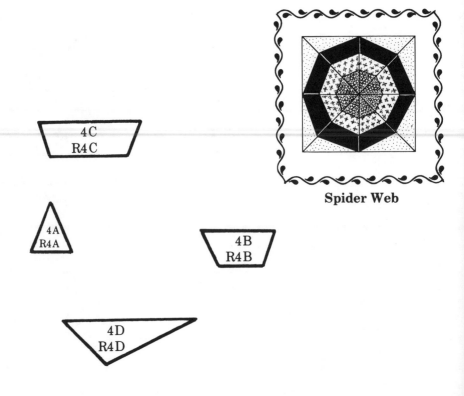

Spider Web

4A
R4A

4B
R4B

4D
R4D

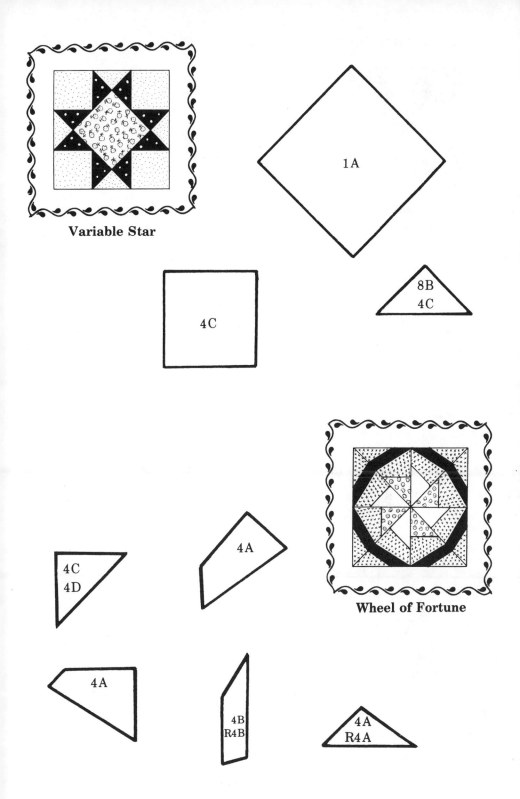

Variable Star

1A

8B
4C

4C

Wheel of Fortune

4C
4D

4A

4A

4B
R4B

4A
R4A

Whirlpool

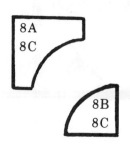

8A
8C

8B
8C

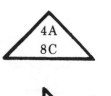

4A
8C

8A
R8A
8B
R8B

4C

Wood Lily

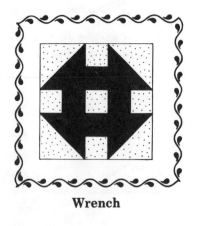

Wrench

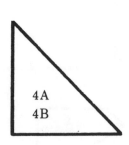

4A
4B

5B
4A

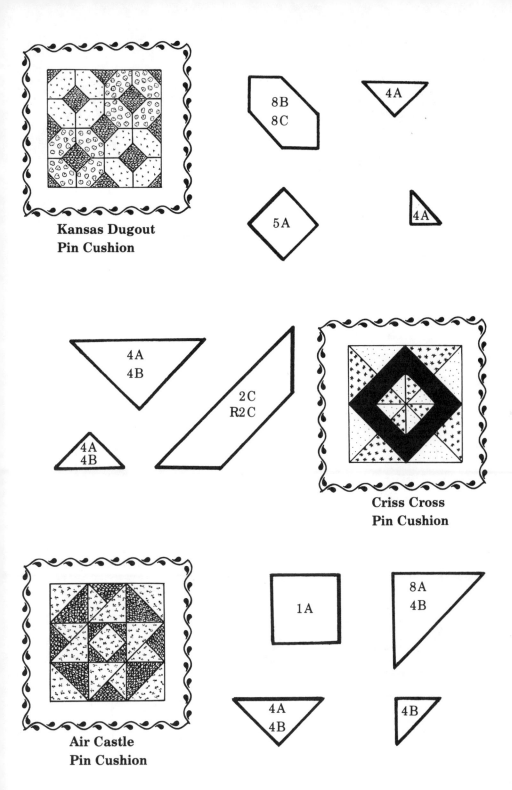

**Kansas Dugout
Pin Cushion**

8B
8C

4A

5A

4A

4A
4B

4A
4B

2C
R2C

**Criss Cross
Pin Cushion**

1A

8A
4B

4A
4B

4B

**Air Castle
Pin Cushion**

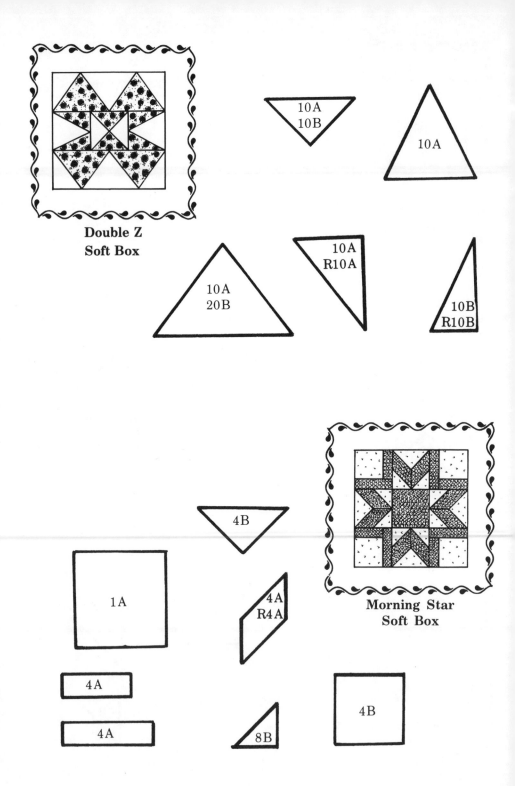

**Double Z
Soft Box**

10A
10B

10A

10A
R10A

10A
20B

10B
R10B

4B

**Morning Star
Soft Box**

1A

4A
R4A

4A

4A

8B

4B

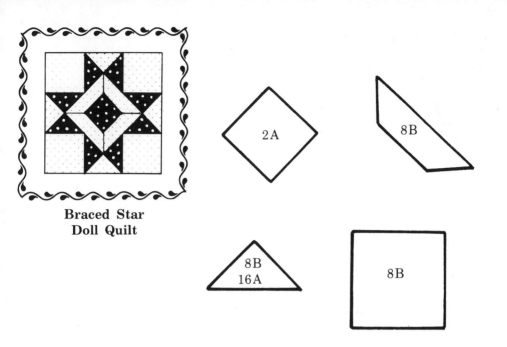

**Braced Star
Doll Quilt**

2A

8B

8B
16A

8B

**Shooting Star
Doll Quilt**

72B

144C

144A

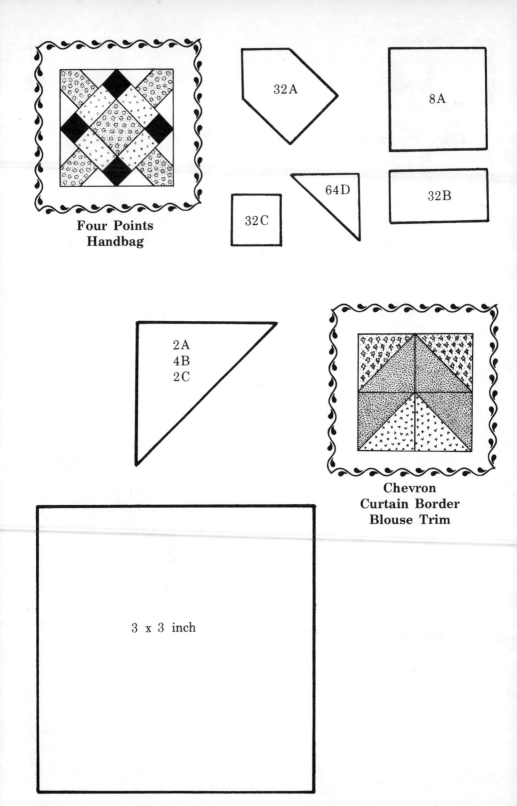

Four Points
Handbag

32A

8A

64D

32C

32B

2A
4B
2C

Chevron
Curtain Border
Blouse Trim

3 x 3 inch